Kia Ora New Zealand

By Sohan Chunduru
Illustrated by Katarina Stevanović

Library of Congress cataloging in process

ISBN: 978-1-64153-389-8

Acknowledgements

I want to thank Ms. Stewart, who is such a kind and caring advisor for the Student Leadership Diversity Committee at LJCDS of which I am a proud member, for broadening my worldview and appreciation of different cultures. I am lucky to have you in my life.

I am grateful to Mr. David Downs of New Zealand for trusting me with conducting research on museums and introducing me to the wonders of MOTAT. Thank you for giving me this wonderful opportunity.

Join Gigi and Geoff as they leave on a tour.
It's a marathon journey, and that's for sure.
They're off to a country that's simply terrific,
located way down in the southern Pacific.

New Zealand's a nation of mountains and fjords,
with north and south islands, so fun to explore.
Its history is Maori and British, you'll find.
But call the folks Kiwis; they really don't mind.

In the city of Auckland, the children are met
by a Maori greeting they'll never forget.
The hongi is something that Maoris do,
but seems quite exotic to me and to you.

They start with "Kia Ora," which just means hello.
Then for doing the hongi here's what you should know.
It's a tribal tradition for girls and for guys.
You gently touch noses while closing your eyes.

Now Gigi and Geoff make a plan for the day.
With so much to see, there's no time for delay.
So they look at their map and head off to the station,
where they hop on a train to their first destination.

Rotorua was built by a volcanic lake
in an area likely to quiver and quake.
And the lava contained in the earth down below
can often create a spectacular show.

There are bubbling mud pools and sizzling streams
and geysers exploding with water and steam.
And mineral springs that are gushing and hot.
And the children agree that they like it a lot.

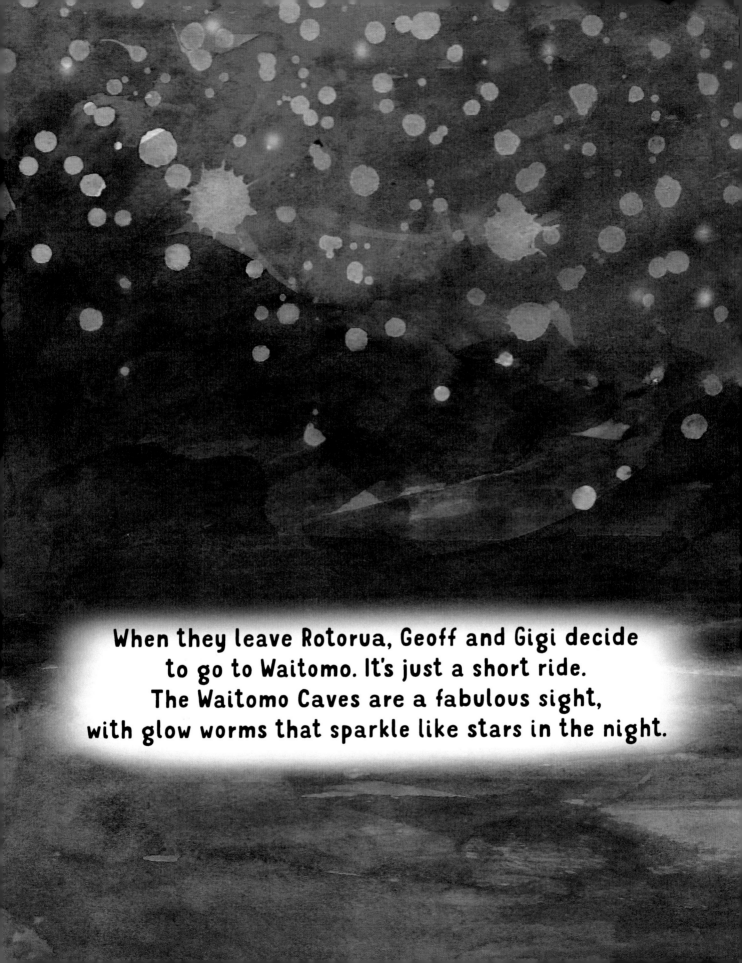

When they leave Rotorua, Geoff and Gigi decide
to go to Waitomo. It's just a short ride.
The Waitomo Caves are a fabulous sight,
with glow worms that sparkle like stars in the night.

Though truth to be told, they're not glow worms at all.
They're the larvae of flies on the ceilings and walls.
So why do they glitter and twinkle this way?
It's a trick that can help them to capture their prey.

When it reaches midday, Geoff and Gigi get lunch
in a kiwi café where there's plenty to munch.
They choose from a menu of seafood and lamb,
and something called Manuka honey-cured ham.

For dessert, they have Lolly Cake, Jelly Tips too,
and a sweet, creamy donut that's covered in goo.
Then they sit and eat ice cream and drink lemonade
till they leave for a town where some movies were made.

Hobbiton's famous for one single thing.
It's the place where they filmed all the Lord of the Rings,
and the stories of Hobbits you've seen on TV.
And the sets are still standing for people to see.

You can visit Bag End in this magical land,
where Frodo and Bilbo's adventures began.
From the holes of the Hobbits to Green Dragon Inn,
you just open the door, and they welcome you in.

Now, Queenstown is next on this New Zealand break.
It's on the South Island and sits by a lake.
There are many adventurous things you can do,
like hiking and biking, and paddling canoes.

You can jump off a platform they've built up so high
and hope that your bungee will hold as you fly.
There are ziplines for sliding and mountains to climb.
And Gigi and Geoff have a wonderful time.

They head back to Auckland to finish their tour.
It's time to go home, but they want to see more.
So they spend their last day in this beautiful city
where the harbors and hills are incredibly pretty.

They visit the Museum of Transport and Tech,
where they hop on a tram and ride on the deck.
The captain delights them with mariner's tales
of a place that is known as the City of Sails.

Then, at last, it is time for final goodbyes,
as Gigi and Geoff soar through the skies.
Though their love for New Zealand will always remain.
And one day, who knows, they might come back again.

Gigi and Geoff enjoyed their visit to New Zealand.
Would you like to visit someday?

Made in the USA
Middletown, DE
01 April 2025

73637097R00026